GETTING PAID TO
Make Games
and Apps

KRISTINA LYN HEITKAMP

ROSEN
PUBLISHING

New York

Published in 2017 by The Rosen Publishing Group, Inc.
29 East 21st Street, New York, NY 10010

Library of Congress Cataloging-in-Publication Data

Names: Heitkamp, Kristina Lyn, author.
Title: Getting paid to make games and apps / Kristina Lyn Heitkamp.
Description: First edition. | New York : Rosen Publishing, 2017. | Series: Turning your tech hobbies into a career | Audience: Grades 7 to 12. | Includes bibliographical references and index.
Identifiers: LCCN 2016020443 | ISBN 9781508172963 (library bound)
Subjects: LCSH: Computer programming—Vocational guidance—Juvenile literature. | Application software—Juvenile literature. | Computer games—Design—Juvenile literature.
Classification: LCC QA76.6 .H4515 2017 | DDC 005.1023—dc23
LC record available at https://lccn.loc.gov/2016020443

Manufactured in Malaysia

Contents

Introduction

Digital media has become a staple in every household across the world. Games and apps, in particular, have gone viral. It is hard to imagine a day without using a single application or not doing some sort of gameplay because apps make daily life a little bit easier. Like tiny toolkits in our pockets and purses, handy apps can forecast the local weather or help train a budding athlete. They allow a player to define skill sets, explore areas unknown, and connect with people across the world.

Games and apps have also made their way into education, health care, and even environmental activism. Doctors use apps to monitor a patient's heartbeat. Teachers employ games to teach biology, math, and history. Fitness tracker apps challenge laziness and motivate people to move beyond the couch. Some apps help train pets to sit, stay, and roll over.

In the near future, software applications may become the brains of driverless cars, or may be used to fight climate change. The possible applications for connectivity in games and apps stretch far and wide.

Apps can be used on several devices, such as Smart TVs. Users can select favorite films to watch, video conference with friends, or listen to music from one device.

If you already enjoy playing games and using apps, there are many ways to transition your hobby into a career, whether it's by building an app that will be used to teach kids to write code, or creating a game that encourages reduced water consumption and pollution, or anything else you can think of.

Chapter ONE

All Fun and Games

Games and apps are an intrinsic part of our everyday lives. Our world is full of push notifications, software updates, and leveling up. At some point while beak-deep in a game of *Angry Birds*, you may have wondered what it takes to make a game. Or maybe you have a big idea for the next killer app. But in order to turn a hobby of using games and apps into a career, we must first understand what they are and how they are used.

YOU'VE GOT GAME!

A lot of people play games. In 2015, 155 million Americans reported that they play video games. Games connect a diverse global audience of players, bridging different backgrounds, gender, age, and socioeconomic status. But what exactly is a game? Defining games can be a little tricky. *Monopoly, Minecraft, Tetris, World of Warcraft*, and *Pacman* are just some examples, and a list that names all games would extend for well beyond ten pages. Games come in all shapes and sizes, but most games share the same defining traits: a goal, rules, conflict, and freedom to play.

In a game, a player works towards a goal, whether it is filling his or her virtual house full of cats in the popular *Neko Atsume*, or scoring the highest word points in *Words with Friends*. The goal keeps the user motivated and focused on the game. A player can spend hours or days working towards a goal.

Rules are limits on how the player can work towards the goal. Rules challenge the user to explore news ways of getting things done. Obstacles or challenges that occur during gameplay, such as an attack from an opposing player you're attempting to beat or roving monster you're struggling to avoid, are examples of conflict. Players actively participate while following rules, avoiding conflict, and working towards the goal.

Anyone who joins a game knowingly and willingly accepts the goals and rules. The freedom to play or not to play establishes a common ground with other players. Users are free to leave or enter at any time. However, if the player is not entertained, he or she might give up and walk away. A game can have simple goals, rules, and graphics, but if it's engaging, a player can live in the game's world for hours. A great example is *Minecraft*. This block-building game with simple graphics was the fifth best selling video game in 2014, beating out *Mario Kart's* fast-paced and amazing graphics. An engaging game offers immediate satisfying feedback that keeps players coming back for more.

The top devices or platforms that gamers use to play games are personal computers, gaming consoles such as PlayStation 4, smartphones or tablets, and handheld systems such as Nintendo's

At the Virtual Reality Los Angeles Expo, a man tries virtual glasses headset. Virtual reality games include puzzles, action, and sports.

Game Boy. Computer games, video games, console games, and mobile games are all essentially the same form of entertainment, but vary depending on the device on which they are played. There are several different types of games, but most fall into the following categories: action, shooter, role-play, adventure, sports, simulation, strategy, and puzzle. The top three types of video games that gamers play are social games, action, and strategy games. It's hard finding an exact definition of games, but one thing is certain: they continue to grow in popularity. Opportunities to jump into the game industry are plenty.

It's in Our DNA to Play

Once upon a time, the Kingdom of Lydia was troubled. Times were hard and food was scarce. But the Lydians persevered by creating a plan to fight hunger. One day they would eat, and the following day they would not eat. The day without food became a game day. Instead of feeding their bodies, Lydians indulged in games. Playing games all day kept the hungry thoughts at bay. Days with dinner, the game boards were put away. They survived eighteen years of famine on this schedule, so the story goes. Greek storyteller and historian Herodotus included the tale in *The Histories* written in 440 BCE.

Humans have been playing games for a long, long time. Early archeological evidence of different gameplay comes from many places. Dice games are some of the oldest, and the gaming pieces have been found in Turkey, Egypt, and China. The Greeks and Romans engaged in the game of Knucklebones, probably what the Lydians played. It was executed differently depending on the player's age and gender. Kids would simply throw the pieces into the air and try to catch as many as possible on the back of one hand. Unmarried women played Knucklebones to solicit Aphrodite, the Greek goddess of love. The game of chess is another oldie, but goodie. It has been played for centuries all over the world. Chess was used in the Middle Ages to teach aristocrats the strategies of war. Early games share many of the same elements found in games today, like rules and goals. Game platforms have changed since the days of our ancestors, but we are still playing strong.

THERE'S AN APP FOR THIS, THAT, AND EVERYTHING

There's an app for just about everything and everyone. In 2015, over 3 million apps were available for download. There are flash cards apps for toddlers that teach the names of animals, foods, and letters in 13 different languages. Or there are math adventure apps in which the user tutors a monster in division to help him

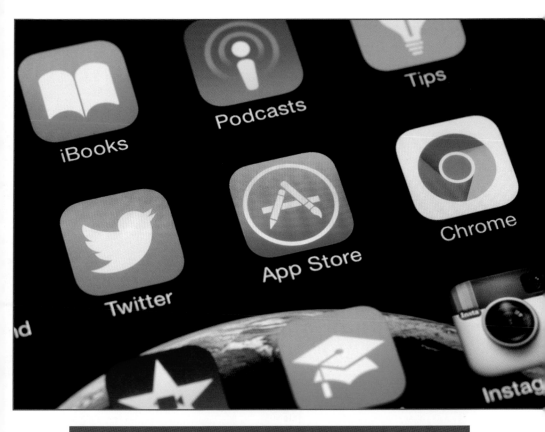

Apps can be downloaded onto a smartphone from an app store, such as Apple App Store or Google Play. Apps are free or available to purchase for a small fee.

battle enemies. There is even an app game that teaches transit safety called *Dumb Ways to Die*. Over a million users gave it a five star rating.

But what exactly is an app? Short for application, apps are software that allows a user to perform a specific task, like listening to music or getting driving directions. Apps can be downloaded from the internet onto your smartphone, tablet, or computer.

Desktop apps are used on a computer. Typical desktop apps include word processors like Microsoft Word, web browsers such as Firefox or Google Chrome, and gadget or widget apps that display handy things like calendars or calculators. Desktop apps are installed on the

From Taiwan's Happy Soul independent game development team, Four Pigs Soccer game app is a four-player soccer game where each person aims to score a goal.

computer either by downloading the software from the internet or inserting an installation disc or flash drive.

The apps found on a smartphone or tablet usually come in three different formats: web app, native app, and hybrid app. Web apps are browser-based and are built like a tiny website. They are retrieved through the internet. The user can access a web app without installing any software, leaving behind those pesky software updates. Web apps can be easier to build but cannot be sold in app stores such as Google Play or Apple App Store.

Native apps are specific to an operating system and platform. An iPhone app will only work on an Apple device, and an Android app will only work on an Android device. Native apps are purchased or installed through an application store, like the Apple App Store or Google Play. Native apps tend to be easier to use and have a faster performance and better reliability than a web app.

Hybrid apps are a combination of web and native apps. A hybrid app is built like a web app but it's translated through a native app. If you have previous experience developing websites, building a hybrid app may be the way to go. Reuse your existing skills without getting locked into platform specific programming languages. Hybrid apps can be distributed in the various app stores. However, hybrid apps can sometimes be unreliable and unresponsive.

If you decide to build a native or hybrid app for an Android or Apple, the process of building and publishing are different. Google Play offers checklists for preparing your app to launch in its store. Apple also provides an App Distribution Guide that includes tips about testing and debugging. Publishing fees are associated with both platforms, but Apple is more costly than Android services.

Tom the Carrot

By the time he was 12 years old, Thomas Suarez had given a TED talk, published two apps, and started his own company. Inspired by Steve Jobs, Suarez started playing around with programming languages when he was nine. He is completely self-taught and says it's frustrating that there aren't more opportunities for young kids to learn programming.

The first app Suarez built is called *Earth Fortune*. The app displays a daily horoscope with a matching color picture of Earth. Next Suarez created the very successful smartphone game called *Bustin Jieber*. Just like a whack-a-mole game, the player tries to catch the tiny face of singer Justin Bieber while he quickly wanders the screen. Both apps are available in app stores.

Suarez's company CarrotCorp makes apps for Apple, Android, and Google Glass. But he hasn't stopped there. In 2015, Suarez announced his prototype for a rotating 3D printer called ORB. The printer is based on the open-source software Arduino. The code is easy to read, and is broken down into building blocks for simple customization. The ORB prints on a fast spinning disc, allowing it print up to ten times faster than other 3D printers. Suarez continues to innovate and explore technology development. His story and success inspires young developers everywhere.

Paying attention to what apps are popular is important if you decide to turn your hobby into a career. What app could you and your friends not live without? To find inspiration for an app idea, do a little crowdsourcing and ask what is missing from the app world. Discover problems that need an app fix. Browse apps stores and take a close look at the top-rated apps. On the flip side, studying bad apps can help you see what doesn't work. Successful apps often have a clean design, are easy to use, and run smoothly. Some popular apps provide a solution to a common problem, while other trendy apps just scratch an itch to have a little fun and be entertaining.

TWO (OR MORE) CAN PLAY AT THIS GAME

Application downloads have steadily increased year after year. In 2009, worldwide app downloads numbered over two billion. In 2014, that number reached 179 billion. The user base is constantly growing, and the app industry is a strong one. There are several opportunities to develop an app, sell it, and become successful.

One person or several people, depending on the skill set, can develop an application. Typically most app development teams have an interface designer, a developer, a tester, and a marketer or promoter. The interface designer thinks about how the user interacts with the app and sketches a corresponding design. The developer writes the code, specific for the supporting platform. The tester tests the technology to make sure it works on different devices and catches any software bugs. Promoting the app is something that all team players should be a part of. If you are an independent hard worker who is interested in all of the roles,

The wildly popular simple-graphics game Minecraft is available to play on several platforms including console, personal computer, and mobile devices. It has sold over a million copies.

building an app can easily be a solo mission if you have the right skills and education.

Games account for a large percentage of apps downloaded. Building games is a bit more complicated than creating a task-oriented application. Depending on the platform, creating a game can take a team of people to build a complicated, graphics-heavy computer game or a fast-paced console game. However, a simple but engaging game app can be built as a solo mission. To set yourself up for success in the booming tech industry, you will need to acquire the proper education and develop the necessary skills before plunging into the competitive and growing field of games and apps.

Chapter TWO

Go to the Head of the Class

The average gamer in the United States clocks six hours a day playing games. If you're one of those gamers, congratulations! Through your hours of play, you probably intuit what works in a game and what does not. Game play provides opportunities to analyze storylines, graphics, rules, and feedback. Player experience will help during the process of building a game or app. But playing isn't enough to turn a hobby into a career. It is a great place to start, but education will supplement your hours of gaming experience.

COVERING A LOT OF GROUND

Exploring education opportunities can happen right inside your school. Sign up for any computer science classes that your school offers. If nothing more specialized than general computer literacy classes is available, don't lose hope. There are many parts to building games. Enroll in creative writing classes to understand the different parts of a good story. A game designer will create an engaging narrative with a feedback system, as well as a script for the cast of characters inside the game. English or communication classes will help hone your writing skills. When it's time to promote or sell your app or game to the public, the ability to write an engaging press release or articulate why your app is far better than the rest is essential.

Participate in art classes. Concept art is part of the process of building any game. The artist will need drawing skills to translate the narrative told in the game design. Basic art and graphic design classes will familiarize you with the tools used to create a winning design. These classes are the essential starting points for sufficiently informing the creative

A storyboard is a sketch of how to organize a story. Creating a storyboard for a game concept will help you plan and execute your idea.

process of a game or app designer. Interpreting the art into a moving story is essential to producing the app or game, and comes next. If your school offers animation, then jump aboard.

An appealing music design and soundtrack will enhance players' experience and keep them engaged for hours on end. Games offer an avenue for musicians to gain experience composing fun contemporary soundtracks. Take classes in music composition, or learn to play an instrument. Music and sound effects evoke a mood and provide valuable feedback. *Mario Kart's* count down to go sound effect gives the player a timing cue of when to push the pedal to the metal. The sound of collecting coins or rings in games offers a satisfying and rewarding audio cue to the player. It's difficult to imagine playing *The Legend of Zelda* or *Halo* without the sweeping musical scores of adventure and danger. Pay attention to all the different sounds in the world and think about how to incorporate them into your app or game soundtrack.

If you have exhausted all the options offered at school, investigate community classes or online courses. Often local colleges or universities will offer computer, illustration, or music courses to the community for a low cost. Several free online courses are available to learn about game design, graphic art and audio engineering. Massachusetts Institute of Technology's (MIT) OpenCourseWare offers Highlights for High School, a free publication of materials and resources for high school students who are interested in science, technology, engineering and math fields. Students can explore MIT's courses and curriculum, such as game design and video game history. Khan Academy is another open source online education opportunity. Students can learn how to create animations and games. The academy offers instructional videos, practice exercises and lessons in computer programming and several other topics.

Crack the Code

You have just come up with the next killer app concept or best-selling game idea. You're sure that Apple and Nintendo will be knocking on your door, outbidding each other for a piece of your brainchild. But you haven't a clue about coding. Several different coding boot camps are available to give you the necessary background. The camps vary in learning intensity from beginner coding to programming at a professional level. Some camps are offered during the summer for those whose school schedule is already crammed with activities and homework. Regardless, they vary in cost, and scholarships are available for specific programs.

The Code Avenger's Code Camp invites kids ages 10-18 to learn the basics of coding games, apps, and websites with other code campers. The camp is held in several locations worldwide, and offers free and paid classes. The Make School Summer Academy located in San Francisco, Silicon Valley, and New York City provides a full-time summer program where participants learn code and build iPhone games or apps. Applicants must be at least 13 years of age to attend the academy and be available for the entire camp term. Scholarships are available to help cover tuition. iD Tech Camps have summer day camps and overnight camps for teens. Located on 150 U.S. university campuses, the tech camps teach a wide range of topics from robotics to coding. Students explore life on a college campus and take tours of real-life game and app companies. iD Tech also has an online learning community called Tech Rocket where kids and teens learn code, game design, and graphic design. Through Tech Rocket, free and paid courses are available.

PUT ON YOUR THINKING APP

The basic education needed to build apps is less complicated than building games. Pick a platform—either iPhone or Android—to work in, learn the technical skills, and go! Look into computer science classes that your school offers to learn more about code. Enroll in any business classes available to help with behind-the-scenes stuff like budgeting, promoting, or turning your app building into a business, like Thomas Suarez's Carrot Corp.

If computer science classes are not offered, several online options are available, and most of the classes are free. Microsoft Virtual Academy provides free online courses available to help students learn the latest technology and build their skills. Classes include mobile app development and all the

Sitting down with a piece paper, a pen, and an idea is a great place to start brainstorming for app ideas. Draft the app layout and different elements.

programming languages you will need to build that killer app. Codecademy is another gem in free online education. Their interactive classes teach nine different programming languages such as HTML and JavaScript. The academy's mission is to revamp education with an engaging, fun, and inspiring experience. Add to your playlist with Stanford iTunes. Completely free, users have access to an archive of audio and video educational content from Stanford's different schools and programs. Listen to *How to Start a Startup* seminar given by the business school. Or tune into lectures on developing apps for iPhones and iPads. Pick and chose from several lectures, podcasts, and presentations.

If you're nervous about learning computer science, start with just one hour. The Hour of Code invites tens of millions of students from over 180 different countries. The event is held each year during Computer Science Education Week, but schools can host the event anytime. The event is organized by Code.org, a non-profit committed to making computer science more accessible to everyone, especially women and underrepresented students of color. Hour of Code aims to demystify code and teach anyone the basics. Using computers, smartphones, or tablets, tutorials help students become familiar with code. You won't learn how to build an app in one hour, but if the thought of code makes your brain fuzzy with panic, this event will help you overcome those initial fears or insecurities. If the hour left you wanting more, Code.org offers several free online learning tools and classes for all coding levels.

Other online education opportunities are available, such as Udemy, Lynda, and Code School. These learning platforms can teach users the necessary code to build games and apps. Some of them offer free beginner courses, but most classes charge a fee.

Closing the Gap

According to the Entertainment Software Association, 44 percent of gamers are women. Yet, women fill only 26 percent of computing jobs. The national nonprofit Girls Who Code recognizes the gender gap in technology and is dedicated to doing something about it. Every summer Girls Who Code offers a summer immersion program held in over fifteen different cities across the United States. The participants learn different aspects of computer science, including robotics and mobile app development. The

(continued on the next page)

A student works on an Adobe Systems exercise during a Girls Who Code class in San Jose, California The summer immersion program offers classes in game and app development.

(continued from the previous page)

camps include field trips and guest speakers. Girls leave camp with valuable computer science, leadership, and teamwork skills. No previous coding experience is necessary, and all skill levels are encouraged to apply. The program ends with a final project that you share with campmates. But, here's the best part: the program is free for all participants. Housing and transportation are not included, but there are scholarships available for those in need. To be eligible, you must be a current sophomore or junior in a U.S. high school and be fully committed to the 7-week program.

Andrea Gonzales and Sophie Houser met at the Girls Who Code summer immersion program, and decided to collaborate on the final project. Both girls knew that they wanted to make a game with a social message. After some research they decide to tackle the worldwide stigma of menstruation. They wanted to find a way to eradicate the taboo associated with a very natural and normal occurrence. *The Tampon Run* game app invites players to shoot tampons at enemies to pummel the menstruation taboo. The game app is available in the Apple store.

CHOOSE YOUR WEAPON

Over 400 U.S. universities and colleges offer gaming degrees or certifications. Several programs designed specifically for mobile development are also available. Attaining a formal education will give you the opportunity to connect with other students, tap

Universities, colleges and technical schools in the United States offer degree programs ranging from professional certifications to master's degrees for aspiring game programmers, developers, and designers.

into professors' experience, and tailor the education towards your specific passions. Important to note: If you're going to gain credentials, make sure the program is accredited. Accreditation is a process of validating and evaluating an educational program to ensure it meets a minimum standard.

Certification programs are available in game development, digital art and design production, mobile computing, and much more. Programs consist of classroom time, practical application, and tests. Certifications are usually completed in half the time it takes to earn a two- or four-year degree. Some colleges will allow the credits earned for the certificate to transfer over to a degree if the student chooses to go back for more education. Or, for a relatively inexpensive route to certification, check out Coursera. The educational online platform has partnered with different universities to provide free online classes to anyone. Coursera also offers several specialization programs that include four-to-five classes in one specific area. Master the skills to build an iPhone app with the University of Toronto's specialization program. Or take the five-course game design specialization with the California Institute of the Arts. The program teaches students the fundamentals of crafting a video game design. For the class's final project, called the Capstone Project, students create a game design document that includes narrative, concept, and an outline with the different elements of the game.

If you want a more in-depth education than a certification offers, you can pursue an associate or bachelor's degree, or seek a minor in many different subjects. Some degrees may be held under an all-encompassing title like Game Art, but students can tailor interest with specific classes offered such as 3D design and animation. Take your education even further, and tackle a master's degree or PhD in game design or mobile game design. Michigan State offers a PhD in Media and Information Studies. Students work together with professors in the Games for Entertainment and Learning Lab (GEL) to design innovative games and research how games influence and engage players.

If you would like to get started after high school but are not interested in the college scene, DigiPen Institute of Technology has a precollege program that combines college-level coursework with practical experience. The institute also offers youth programs, including summer, year-round, and online programs that teach just about any aspect of building games. Regardless of where you go or how you get it, taking the steps to gain the education is invaluable to gaining employment in the industry or going out on your own.

Chapter THREE

Skills to Pay the Bills

Armed with a degree or certification, you are now ready to sharpen the skills that will pay the bills. Technical skills, such as reading and writing code or digitally drawing, are essential to successfully turning a hobby into a career. Soft skills, such as maintaining a positive attitude and remaining curious, are also important to a lasting career.

GET WITH THE PROGRAM

There are several parts to building a game and many opportunities to learn the different skills needed to bring a game idea to the world of players. From coding to sound engineering, various programs are available to learn the skills. The programs are a great way to play around with the technology and discover if it's a good fit for you.

Some professional game designers suggest that regardless of where you land in the field of game development, all parts

Programming languages offer different tools for different jobs. However, they do have certain similarities that will make learning more than one easier.

of the team should have basic code knowledge. If you want to build a game, you've got to know how to speak the language. Just as an architect wouldn't use cooking instructions to build a house, game designers use specific coding languages for the games they build. The programming language a developer will use varies depending on if the gaming platform is a smartphone, desktop, or console. Android games use Java or C++. Games built for iPhone or iPad use Objective-C or Swift. Computer games usually use Java, C++, or C#. Whatever platform you choose, having the knowledge of one coding language will help you more easily learn others.

The Enchantress of Numbers

Daughter of the notable Romantic poet Lord Byron, Ada Lovelace was born in 1815 in London, England. Shortly after her birth, her parents' marriage took a nosedive and Lord Byron left England, his daughter Ada, and his mathematician wife Lady Byron. She worried that Ada would follow her father's path of poetry and romanticism. Lady Bryon insisted that her daughter learn the world of mathematics and sciences, which was unusual for a woman in nineteenth-century England. She hoped to squash any romantic ideals that Ada may have inherited from her father. Ada was a curious and inventive little girl. When she was 12 years old, she drafted up a flying machine based on her observations of birds and the mechanics of flying.

When Ada was 17 years old, she met Charles Babbage at a dinner party. The mathematician captivated Ada with his new calculating engine, the Analytical Engine. Years later, Ada published a translation of an article written about the engine, and included her own notes about the calculating machine. She predicted that it might be used for both

(continued on the next page)

Ada Lovelace was a brilliant mathematician who also learned music and drawing and was fluent in French. She often used metaphor and imagination to evaluate scientific ideas.

(continued from the previous page)

practical and scientific applications. Ada thought that the machine could rearrange symbols with regard to certain rules and logic to produce anything from words to complex music— essentially what a computer program does today. Turns out she was correct, but scholars did not discover this until well after Ada's death. Ada Lovelace is recognized a the first computer programmer. The software language developed by the U.S. Department of Defense was named Ada in her honor. Ada programming language is used in high-security systems for military aircraft, railroad systems, and medical devices.

Perhaps the strange-sounding language names give you anxiety. Or maybe you're worried about spending time learning a language to ultimately discover you don't like building games. Accessible educational code programs are available that will allow you to try before you buy with your time, such as Scratch or Game Maker. Developed by MIT students, Scratch is an open-source introductory code program. The user can create animations, games, or interactive stories with the program's basic building block format. Several tutorials are available on the program's website and on YouTube. Game Maker Studio helps a beginner build a game with easy dragging and dropping game development. Without having to write a single line of code, the user can have a game ready for play very quickly. Game Maker Studio is free to download, but is resource-limited, and does not include access to all the features.

If you are ready to level up after testing the beginner programs, move on to more advanced game development tools, such as Unity. Learn code as you build games with Unity. Create cross-platform 2D or 3D games with Unity's free personal edition. Several tutorials, video and written manuals, and live Q&A sessions are available for free on their website. Unity is often a favorite with indie game studios for two reasons: the professional edition is relatively inexpensive, and games can be sold across several different mobile, desktop, and console platforms. However, the game engine is also popular with large game development companies. A few well-known and popular games built with Unity are *Battlestar Galactica Online, Assassin's Creed Identity*, and the puzzle game, *Escape Plan*. If you enjoy learning the fundamentals of Unity, they offer a developer certification program that teaches a plethora of skills, such as game art principles and audio effects and properties.

An engaging game becomes more interesting with attractive graphics and appealing music. Amazing eye candy and emotional music will enhance the gameplay experience and captivate the player. To create beautiful graphics and animations, you will need to be familiar with certain tools. Open-source Inkscape software can create professional quality vector graphics. Several written and video tutorials are available to learn the program's many features. The active Inkscape community also guides new users and provides helpful tips and feedback. GIMP is another valuable tool. The free and open program is used to edit photos and manipulate images or free-form drawing. Or, bring your images to life with the 3D animation open-source software Blender. With the 3D creation suite, you can model, simulate, animate, and even make games. It may take time to learn the ropes, but once you understand all the tools found in Blender, it will be worth it.

Music or sound affects provide valuable feedback to the player and can help keep the user emotionally engaged. Several websites provide open-source sound affects or music that you can incorporate into a game project. Or if you prefer to make your own music or effects, use Audacity, a free, cross-platform audio editing software. It can be used to record live or computer audio and edit the track. You can slice, splice, copy, and mix sounds.

DO NOT PASS GO WITHOUT THESE SKILLS

With the right skills, you can break into app development all by yourself. Programs are available that make it easy to build an app, test it, and send it out to the app market. After defining the goal of the app and researching similar apps, the next step is to sketch the structure and design. To help visualize the user interface, the free and easy-to-use online tool Frame Box will help get the job done. Frame Box lets you mock-up the app concept with different drag-and-drop elements. Draft it up and send to friends for feedback.

Created in open-source Inkscape software, the apple has a stained glass effect. Inkscape can be used to design and edit graphics for your game.

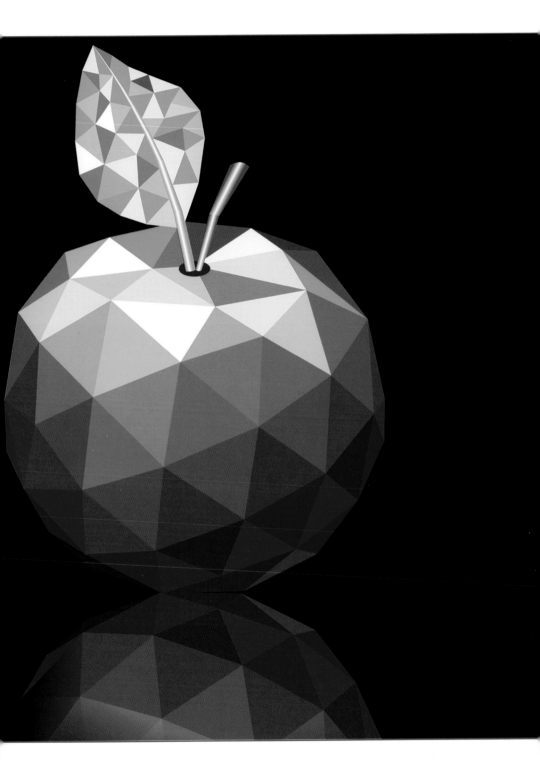

After the concept and design are configured, it's time for coding. App building software programs are available that will do all the coding for you. The Android App Inventor is a project of MIT that seeks to bring software development to all people. It is free and easy to use. Using the accessible interface, simply drag and drop building blocks to create an app without writing a single line of code. The Inventor creates native apps specifically for Androids. Or if you want to learn the language of Android apps, Java is the official programming language for Android

The popular gaming app *Angry Birds* was first created for Apple iPhones, and later for other devices such as Android, tablets and gaming consoles.

development. Several free online classes are available, such as Codecademy or Learn Java Online.

With Apple's Xcode, you can build apps for iPhone, iPad, Apple Watch, and even Apple TV. The program also employs a drag-and-drop user interface, making the code easy to read and write. Apple apps use Objective-C or Swift language. Video and written tutorials are available to learn both Swift and Objective-C languages. In order to sell your app in the Apple App Store, you will need to sign up for Apple's Developer Program and pay the yearly membership fee. The program offers tools, resources, and a testing ground for the app. However, you have to be at least 18 years old to join. It is possible to join under a parent or guardian's name, and they will be responsible for any income taxes associated with the money made from selling your app.

PLAYING WITH A FULL DECK

Technical education and skills will supply you with the tools to make a game or app. But to step beyond the backroom techie bubble of coding and into the role of business partner or owner, you will need valuable soft skills.

Communication is one of the top-scoring soft skills to have in any field, career, or position. If you cannot effectively communicate, then you may as well be speaking a prehistoric language of grunts and shrugs. Translating a game concept or design to your team is imperative. Also the ability to honestly and respectfully talk with your team members will help with navigating through difficult conversations, such as receiving strong opinions or having disagreements.

Curiosity is another high scorer. The ability to remain curious means staying up to date on all the latest technology and

Two heads are better than one. Collaboration can lead to creative learning, resourceful solutions, and innovative ideas.

modern platforms and keeping an eye out for the next big idea. Perseverance goes hand-in-hand with curiosity. Having the courage and guts to keep moving can be difficult, but it is very important to achieving success. If at first you don't succeed, ask why and then try again. Curiosity leads to creativity and creativity leads to innovation.

Another contender for a top-scoring soft skill is collaboration. Whether you're venturing out on a solo game development mission or joining forces with an established team, negotiating and working well with others is crucial. Willingness to give and receive feedback gracefully and respectfully is imperative. Finally, having a positive attitude scores major bonus points. When times get hard, and you can't quite figure out why your game or app is bugged or why it's not selling, having a positive attitude will build you up and keep you going, giving you extra life to power up through any challenge.

Chapter FOUR

Show Me Your Moves

The U.S. Department of Labor reports that by the year 2020, there will be 1.4 million computer specialist job openings, but only 400,000 computer science students to fill them. The tech industry is practically begging for more applicants. The future is bright and open with possibilities.

PAID TO PLAY

The game industry, in particular, offers a range of diverse positions, from game designers to sound engineers or graphic artists. GameJobs, GameIndusty.biz, and Gamasutra are all excellent places to find jobs specific to your locale or expertise. Development companies, headhunting firms, industry analysts, and retailers all use these job sites to discover budding talent. Research different positions to get a sense of preferred qualifications or job requirements. Then, post your resume there,

The German game company Deck13 team consists of game designers, concept artists, and 2D and 3D designers. Deck13 was awarded Studio of the Year at the German Development Awards 2014.

or set up job alerts. These sites also offer industry news and advice from experts in different fields.

A unique alternative to the traditional route of finding a job is the App Academy. Students dive deep into app development education without paying a dime of tuition upfront in this 12-week immersive program. Successfully graduated App Academy students pay the education bill after graduation, and more importantly, after they've scored a developer job. Applicants must complete coding exercises, pass an entrance exam, and interview over the phone. Prior programming experience will

(continued from the previous page)

to dig into the minds of Apple's engineers and experts. New products are shared and diverse new friendships formed. Scholarships are available for students 13 years or older. If you can't make it, videos of the previous events are available to watch. Google offers a similar developer conference in California every year called Google I/O. The two-day event features workshops, product demos, and tech sessions on all the latest Android technologies. Academic admission tickets are available for a fraction of the general admission price. To qualify for the limited academic tickets you must be an active full-time student in high school or college. Live-streaming videos are available on the event's webpage or on YouTube after the conference.

as was mentioned before, reach can be limited because the coding language you choose will determine which platforms will support your app. If you created an iOS App, you can only sell it in Apple's App Store. There, your app will face fierce competition, considering that there are over a million apps available for download. Usually only the most popular apps are featured, so getting exposure for a new app is difficult. For Android apps, the market place is varied, from Google Play to Amazon and Blackberry. In addition to the fees that allow you to place your app in an app store is the commission that app stores take. Usually, it is 30 percent of your app revenues. Weigh the entry and operating costs against possibilities of exposure carefully, but know that you're paying to be a part of a huge marketplace and distribution channel that is like no other.

Indie game or app development takes focus, resourcefulness, and self-reliance. Building your own business means handling the budget and financial planning.

Independent video games, or indie games, are video games developed by individuals or small teams without any financial support from game publishers or developers. Indie game developers have no creative limitations because they don't have to answer to an investor. Indie game developers are also uninvolved with publishers who would otherwise take anywhere from 25 to 50 percent of revenues. However, indie game developers have to find their own funding. Publishers often finance the development of the game and have a far-reaching hand for distribution. However, several resources are available to raise money for an indie game, such as crowdfunding, which is funding a project by raising small increments of money from several people. Depending on the game's platform (mobile app game, web game, or console), the indie team may be able to distribute the game through digital distribution.

There are many games and apps available, but users have limited space on their mobile phones or tablets. Building a good app or game will offer sufficient reason to let what you created take up that space. Invest in making the best version. Earn trust from your user by reading reviews and ratings, and listening to feedback. Address the issues or suggestions. Your game or app will need to outperform the other well-known and trusted apps.

The Electronic Entertainment Expo is an annual game trade show held in Los Angeles. Notable attendees include major players such as Xbox.

Once it's as good as it could possibly be, it's time to get the word out about your app with the help of reviews, bloggers, and magazine write-ups. Because if no one has a means of discovering your app, then they wont know to download and use it. Develop your app pitch to perfection. This pitch, also called an elevator pitch, is a short description of your app highlighting what makes it stand out from the rest. Another fun way to announce your game or app is to create a trailer, or more simply put, a video advertisement. Take screen shots of your app, write a short script describing its functions, and find open-source music to tie it all together. Several free editing and publishing tools are available, such as YouTube, Vimeo, and Vine. Utilize social media outlets to help with publicity, and be sure to be welcoming of a global audience. By 2020, 70 percent of the world's population, or about 5.4 billion people, will use smartphones.

NOT THE ONLY GAME IN TOWN

Game designer and app developer are not the only career options in the tech industry. Maybe code is not your thing, or you're more interested in discovering the next best game to play or app to use. Many roles are available in game and app development, from producer to voice actor.

If you're a natural-born leader with exceptional organizational skills, a producer or project manager position may be a good fit. The producer or project manager oversees the game or app project and is responsible for many tasks, such as handling budget goals, setting deadlines, taking care of contracts, and managing the project teams. The producer is detail oriented, and a people person. But first and foremost, he or she must have a passion for games that will offer motivation during stressful late-night hours.

Tech Dreams Come True

After downloading an Apple app, Nick D'Aloisio was curious about how applications were built. As a result, he taught himself how to code at the age of 12, with the hopes of reaching his goal of eventually developing his own app idea. Every app he developed was a learning exercise, and through trial and error, he got better and better at it.

At 15 years old, D'Aloisio developed a prototype for a digital content summarizing app called Trimit. It condensed massive amounts of information into bite-size digestible chunks. The app quickly caught the attention of investors. D'Aloisio was given venture capital funding, which is money provided by investors for startups or projects. He started on re-designing Trimit and turned it into the popular app Summly. The app gathered news articles based on selected interests. It summarized key points of selected articles in just a few sentences, keeping the app user up-to-date on all the latest news. Summly became very popular with over 200,000 downloads and was chosen as the App of the Week by Apple. In 2013, Yahoo purchased Summly for a reported $30 million. After that, D'Aloisio went to work for Yahoo. A year later, in 2014, he announced a new app called Yahoo News Digest— an evolved version of Summly. It was the winner of the 2014 Apple Design Award. He continues to innovate and learn. When he turned 18 years old, D'Aloisio took a break from working at Yahoo to focus on computer science and philosophy degrees at Oxford University in England.

Testers try out the product before it is made available to the public. Testers are paid to play over and over again to catch any glitches, and make sure the game works across different platforms. Attention to detail, experience playing a range of games, and the ability to articulate and communicate the issues are all important skills to have when going for the job role as a tester. Patience is required when playing a game over and over, especially if the game is not one's game of choice.

Or, if you are the go-to person for advice on the newest app or game, consider a career as a tech journalist or reviewer that offers the world of users advice. Find new and interesting apps and games and try them out, and publish a review on your blog or

Leading the team to success, a project manager answers questions and helps navigate challenges related to timelines, deliverables, and contracts.

website and share with the world. Ask your audience what they look for in games, and review games you think will promise or disappoint users. But be sure to remain objective, and try not to slide into a demeaning attitude. A tech journalist's job is not to crush the game developer's spirit, but to provide feedback.

Another of many options is voice acting. With every great game, a scripted dialogue is shared among the gaming characters. Voice actors are needed to bring the game's narrative to life, and this role offers an opportunity to let the actor share his or her dramatic side.

Chapter FIVE

Future of the Industry

F rom Knucklebones to Minecraft, games have been played for thousands of years and probably will be played for thousands more. Applications are a newer technology, but they have become

More than half of gamers play with others, including friends and family members. Games have become a key source of social entertainment.

an essential part of how we interact with the world. Games and apps are changing lives one download at a time.

REBOOTING EDUCATION

Video games and apps are shaking up and rebooting traditional education. Even the U.S. Department of Education recommends that teachers, game designers, and developers collaborate to create learning games that engage students. Kids already spend a lot of time playing games so why not channel that interest to history, science, and math lessons in a game format? *Minecraft: Education Edition* lets students explore real world places like ancient Pompeii or the Great Pyramids of Giza. MIT's Games for Learning program is supplying teachers with educational interactive games to play in and outside the classroom. In *Radix Endeavour*, students explore a virtual ecosystem, examining animal poop to diagram connections between plants and animal diet. Learning biology has never been so much fun! Another game called *Lure of Labyrinth* teaches students pre-algebra while they protect the world from monsters and save lost pets. Players have found more than 30 million virtual pets by using their math skills.

A New York school only uses game-based learning in their classrooms. Quest to Learn is a public middle and high school that believes a technology-rich environment empowers students to invent their future. Teachers teach all the common core subjects through interactive digital or analog games. Ninth graders learn biology by spending a year as a scientist in a fictional biotech company, cloning dinosaurs and creating a stable ecosystem for them. Through role-play, students learn biology, genetics, and ecology. *Galactic Mappers* teaches sixth graders physical

High school students participate in a group discussion. Technology can be used in several ways in a classroom, such as taking notes during a group meeting or presenting information.

geography and mapping skills. Students collaborate in teams to create a map of a new alien world. Quest to Learn students are challenged and engaged. Games and apps will continue to be used in classrooms. Educational games are a huge market that is expanding every day with new and inventive ways to activate participation and high engagement.

Jane The Concussion Slayer

Jane McGonigal believes that reality is broken and games will be the thing to fix it. Game designer and author McGonigal advocates using games to solve real-life problems such as anxiety, depression, and even climate change. In 2009, she suffered a debilitating concussion after accidently slamming her head into a cabinet door. After a few months, she had still not recovered. She suffered terrible migraines and extreme mental fogginess. Her world was turned upside down and backwards. She was anxious and depressed and worried that she would never see the light at the end of the tunnel.

McGonigal decided to use her game design skills to create a game called *Super Better*. A multiplayer game, *Super Better* allows a player to set a health or wellness goal and invites other players to help reach the goal. The game, originally titled *Jane the Concussion Slayer*, helped McGonigal during her recovery and has assisted nearly a half million others reach their own wellness goals— whether it's making a physical or athletic breakthrough, or coping with chronic pain.

Since her recovery, McGonigal has been busy writing books, developing games, and serving as the director of Games Research and Development at the Institute for the Future. She is also the founder of Gameful, a secret headquarters for world-changing game developers. But her epic-winning goal is to see a game designer with a Nobel

POWER OF THE APP

Games and apps have changed lives. Some apps make life a little easier by linking the user to valuable information while others help make the world a better place. Social good apps are motivating users to become more socially involved in important issues. The American Red Cross Donor App allows users to find blood drives, schedule appointments, and track blood donation through to delivery. Donors save lives with a simple tap of an app. Another social good app working to save lives is *Spoiler Alert*. In 2104 nearly 50 million American households struggled against hunger. Yet pounds and pounds of edible food rot in landfills. The *Spoiler Alert* app is fighting hunger and food waste by connecting food businesses and farmers with nonprofit organizations to recover valuable food.

Founded in 2004, Games for Change (G4C) is a nonprofit dedicated to leveraging games for social good. G4C understands the power of gaming entertainment and helps create and distribute games that serve a humanitarian and educational effort, such as *Cloud Chasers*. Released in October 2015, *Cloud Chasers-Journey of Hope* invites players to help a father and daughter traverse through a dangerous and deadly desert to the world above the clouds. The mobile game allows players to explore the important topic of migration from a different perspective. The player helps the family manage their resources and persevere towards a better future.

HAPPINESS HACKING

"Play a game and call me in the morning." This may become a common phrase for medical professionals to use in the near

Technology is changing how doctors diagnose, treat, and interact with patients. Doctors can share progress of a patient's recovery or pull up an x-ray on a device.

future. Game and app technology in healthcare is an emerging and profitable market.

Attention deficit hyperactivity disorder (ADHD) is one of the most common childhood disorders, but it also affects adolescents and adults. While drug prescriptions help, researchers discovered that computer games have potential to ease ADHD symptoms, too. *Project: Evo* hopes to help patients with ADHD, autism, Alzheimer's disease, and depression. Neuroscientists developed the concept of the game. Played on a smartphones or tablets, the player roams an interactive, virtual icy world. The goal of the game is to avoid certain objects, such as miniature icebergs, while finding others, such as specific colored fish. As with any technology claiming a fix, skeptics are wary of videogames offering an effective

Akili Interactive Labs aims to build clinically validated assessments, diagnostics, and therapies that look and feel like video games. Akili's team consists of cognitive scientists, medical engineers, and data analysts.

treatment. But the makers of the game, a biotech company called Akili, are treating the game like any prototype for a medical prescription. *Project: Evo* has been through several clinical trials and is seeking FDA approval. Akili aims to develop a new type of what they call "electronic medicine" that can be prescribed by doctors.

A top-selling fitness app is helping users become healthier. *Zombies, Run!* encourages the user to walk, run, or jog anywhere in the world to help rescue other survivors in the zombie apocalypse. With 200 missions to select from, users listen to the story and are prompted to quicken the pace when zombies are near. Another popular app links the user to a network of 100,000 doctors. The *HealthTap* app provides immediate access to top medical experts in over 140 different specialties. Wonder if that itchy bump is a rash or a spider bite? Send questions to the network or schedule a virtual check-up. Tap into a wealth of health knowledge. Because people are living longer, e-health will likely become a staple of the future.

A WHOLE NEW BALL GAME

Games and apps are infiltrating our schools, doctor's offices, and homes. Opportunities to reinvent how we engage in gameplay and how we use apps are revolutionizing education, health care,

and even communication between users and objects. Innovative applications for games and apps are waiting in the corners of creative minds.

With the Internet of Things revolution revving its powerful engine, our world could become a system of connections. The Internet of Things is a connected network of objects that can send and receive important data over the internet. For example, consider a smartwatch or fitness tracker that uses sensors to

Users can connect even their cars to their phones. An automatic parking assistant app can squeeze a car into tight spots without the driver touching the wheel.

monitor movement and then send that data to an interface. After checking the app, you discover that you walked, jogged, or ran 7.8 miles that day. Coding could become a shared universal language. Programmers will be needed to build the apps that will help connect and control the physical world. In the future, one thing is certain: the building blocks for creating games and apps will be valuable and necessary to constructing our connected world. Whether it is creating an app to drive a drone to deliver food to those in need or motivating a player to push beyond her chronic illness, code connects data to real-life applications.

Glossary

accreditation A process of validating and evaluating an educational program to ensure it meets a minimum standard.

app Short for application, this is software that allows a user to perform a specific task.

certification A verification of a person's skill set in a specific subject, such as mobile computing.

code All or parts of the instructions written in a particular programming language, such as Java, Objective-C, or others, that make up a program.

cross-platform Software or hardware that can operate on different or older platforms, such as an app that runs on both Apple and Android devices, or an old game that can be played on a newer console.

crowdfunding Funding a project by raising small increments of money from several people.

elevator pitch A short description of a project that summarizes and highlights what makes it stand out from the rest.

game engine Software used to build and power a game.

graphics An image or illustration used in software, the quality of which is impacted by development choices and settings, and the platform on which the software is used.

indie games Short for independent, video games developed by individuals or small teams without any financial support from game publishers or developers.

Internet of Things A connected network of physical objects that collects data through sensors, and sends and receives data to and from the internet.

native app An application software program that is made for a specific platform.

open source software Computer software or source code that can be used, altered, and distributed to the public.

platform The basic firmware and software on which specific programs, apps, or games operate, such Android OS or Apple iOS for a phone, a video game console, or a various computer OS.

programming language An artificial language that is used to write a program or software that a machine can interpret and execute.

software An instructional data file, or multiple files, that contains one or more programs and relies on computer devices to run.

soundtrack A recording of music or sound effects that accompanies a game or app.

STEM An acronym for the studies of science, technology, engineering, and math.

user interface What a user interacts with in order to utilize a program or software, whether that means using it for its main function, or changing its settings.

venture capital funding Money provided by investors for startups or projects.

For More Information

Code.org
1301 5th Avenue, Suite 1225
Seattle, WA 98101
website: https://code.org/

Code.org is a nonprofit committed to making computer science
more accessible to everyone, especially women and
underrepresented students of color.

DigiPen Project Fun
9931 Willows Road NE
Redmond, WA 98052
(425) 629-5007
website: https://projectfun.digipen.edu/

Project Fun programs encourage students to explore game
design and multimedia production through a fun and
interactive learning environment.

Entertainment Software Association of Canada
130 Spadina Avenue, Suite 408
Toronto, ON M5V 2L4
(416) 620-7171

website: http://theesa.ca/

Entertainment Software Association of Canada is a nonprofit
trade association that represents major video game makers
and developers.

Girls Who Code
28 W. 23rd Street, 4th Floor
New York, NY 10010
(646) 629-9735
website: http://girlswhocode.com/

Girls Who Code strives to encourage, educate and equip girls
    with computer science skills to pursue STEM careers.

Hatch Canada
3453 Yonge Street, 2nd Floor
Toronto ON M4N 2N3
(416) 546-5501
website: https://hatchcanada.com/

Hatch is a Toronto-area school program that teaches kid to
    code.

The Scratch Project
77 Massachusetts Avenue
Cambridge, MA 02139
(617) 253-5960
website: https://scratch.mit.edu/

The Scratch Project is an open-source program developed by
    MIT students that teaches students to build animations,
    games, and interactive stories.

Women in Communications and Technology
116 Lisgar Street, Suite 300
Ottawa, ON K2P 0C2
(800) 361-2978
website: https://www.wct-fct.com/

Women in Communications and Technology is a Canadian
    nonprofit dedicated to the advancement of women in fields
    of technology.

WEBSITES

Because of the changing nature of internet links, Rosen Publishing has developed an online list of websites related to the subject of this book. This site is updated regularly. Please use this link to access this list:

http://www.rosenlinks.com/TTHIC/games

For Further Reading

Beer, Paula. *Hello App Inventor!: Android Programming for Kids and the Rest of Us.* Shelter Island, NY: Manning Publications Company, 2014.

Bjornlund, Lydia. *The History of Video Games.* San Diego, CA: Referencepoint Press Inc, 2014.

Covey, Sean. *The 7 Habits of Highly Effective Teens.* New York, NY: Simon and Schuster, 2014.

Crooks, Clayton. *iPhone Game Development for Teens.* Boston, MA: Cengage Learning, 2013.

Dreskin, Joel. *A Practical Guide to Indie Game Marketing.* New York, NY: CRC Press, 2015.

Glenn, Joshua; Larsen, Elizabeth Foy. *UNBORED Games: Serious Fun for Everyone.* New York, NY: Bloomsbury Publishing, 2014.

Green, Cary J. *Leadership And Soft Skills For Students: Empowered to Succeed in High School, College, And Beyond.* Indianapolis, IN: Dog Ear Publishing, 2015.

Hagler, Gina. *Ada Lovelace.* New York, NY: The Rosen Publishing Group, 2016.

Hulick, Kathryn. *The Economics of a Video Game.* New York, NY: Crabtree Publishing Company, 2014.

La Bella, Laura. *Building Apps.* New York, NY: The Rosen Publishing Group, 2013.

La Bella, Laura. *Careers for Tech Girls in Video Game Development.* New York, NY: The Rosen Publishing Group, 2015.

Mozer, Mindy. *Social Network-Powered Education Opportunities.* New York, NY: The Rosen Publishing Group, 2013.

Richardson, Craig. *Learn to Program with Minecraft: Transform Your World with the Power of Python.* San Francisco, CA: No Starch Press, 2015.

Rogers, Scott. *Level Up! The Guide to Great Video Game Design.* New York, NY: John Wiley & Sons, 2014.

Sainsbury, Matt. *Game Art: Art from 40 Video Games and Interviews with Their Creators.* San Francisco, CA: No Starch Press, 2015.

Sheldon, Lee. *Character Development and Storytelling for Games.* Boston, MA: Cengage Learning, 2014.

Staley, Erin. *Career Building Through Creating Mobile Apps.* New York, NY: The Rosen Publishing Group, 2013.

Sutherland, Adam. *Be a Young Entrepreneur: Be Inspired to Be a Business Whiz.* Hauppauge, NY: Barron's Educational Series, 2016.

Toppo, Greg. *The Game Believes in You: How Digital Play Can Make Our Kids Smarter.* New York, NY: Macmillan, 2015.

Wilkinson, Colin. *Going Live: Launching Your Digital Business.* New York, NY: The Rosen Publishing Group, 2012.

Bibliography

Adams, Susan. "The Top Colleges and Grad Schools To Study Game Design." *Forbes Magazine*, March 25, 2015. http://www.forbes.com/sites/susanadams/2015/03/25/the-top-colleges-and-grad-schools-to-study-game-design/#4cd74a823441.

Croce, Nicholas. *Cool Careers Without College for People Who Love Video Games.* New York, NY: The Rosen Publishing Group, 2007.

Dembosky, April. "Play This Video Game And Call Me In The Morning." Washington, DC: *National Public Radio*, August 17, 2015. (http://www.npr.org/sections/health-shots/2015/08/17/432004332/play-this-video-game-and-call-me-in-the-morning).

Entertainment Software Association. "2015 Sales, Demographics and Usage Data: Essential Facts about the Computer and Video Game Industry." April 2015. (http://www.theesa.com/wp-content/uploads/2015/04/ESA-Essential-Facts-2015.pdf).

Harel, Idit. "Basic Skills or Soft Skills: What Should Be Taught and Tested." *The Huffington Post*, March 20, 2014. http://www.huffingtonpost.com/idit-harel-caperton/basic-skills-or-soft-skil_b_5000684.html.

Gerardi, David. *Careers in the Computer Game Industry.* New York, NY: The Rosen Publishing Group, 2005.

Good, Alexandra. *Knucklebones.* Johns Hopkins Archaeological Museum, 2011. http://archaeologicalmuseum.jhu.edu/the-collection/object-stories/archaeology-of-daily-life/childhood/knucklebones/.

Funk, Joe. *Hot Jobs in Video Games.* New York, NY: Scholastic Inc., 2010.

Kamenetz, Anya. "The Un-College That's Training $100,000 App Developers." Washington, DC: *National Public Radio*, November 3, 2015. (http://www.npr.org/sections/ed/2015/11/03/451999158/the-un-college-thats-training-100-000-app-developers).

Koster, Raph. *Theory of Fun for Game Design.* Newton, MA: O'Reilly Media, Inc., 2013.

Malykhina Elena. "Fact or Fiction?: Video Games Are the Future of Education." *Scientific American*, September 12, 2014. http://www.scientificamerican.com/article/fact-or-fiction-video-games-are-the-future-of-education/.

Metz, Cade. "Code School Udacity Promises Refunds If You Don't Get A Job." *Wired Magazine*, January 13, 2016. http://www.wired.com/2016/01/udacity-coding-courses-guarantee-a-job-or-your-money-back//

McGonigal, Jane. *Reality Is Broken: Why Games Make Us Better and How They Can Change the World.* New York, NY: Penguin, 2011.

Morals, Betsy. "Ada Lovelace, The First Tech Visionary." *New Yorker*, October 15, 2013. http://www.newyorker.com/tech/elements/ada-lovelace-the-first-tech-visionary.

Pagella, Mario Andres. *Making Isometric Social Real-Time Games with HTML5, CSS3, and JavaScript.* Newton, MA: O'Reilly Media, Inc., 2011.

Sainsbury, Matt. *Game Art: Art from 40 Video Games and Interviews with Their Creators.* San Francisco, CA: No Starch Press, 2015.

Saltzman, Marc. "Game Design: Secrets of the Sages— Creating Characters, Storyboarding, and Design Documents." *Gamasutra.* UBM TechWeb, March 15, 2002. http://www.gamasutra.com/view/feature/131414/game_design_secrets_of_the_sages_.php.

Schell, Jesse. *The Art of Game Design: A Book of Lenses.* Boca Raton, FL: CRC Press, 2015.

Suarez, Thomas. "A 12-year-old app developer." TEDx Manhattan Beach. October 2011. (www.ted.com).

Tucker, Ian. "Nick D'Aloisio: 'I dream of a virtual brain. It's coming in 10 or 20 years.'" *The Guardian*, January 12, 2015. https://www.theguardian.com/technology/2015/jan/12/ nick-daloisio-interview-summly-virtual-brain.

Index

ABOUT THE AUTHOR

Kristina Lyn Heitkamp is a Montana-based writer, researcher, and environmental journalist. She earned a bachelor of arts in English from the University of Utah and a master's of arts in environmental science and natural resource journalism from the University of Montana. Kristina is a freelance researcher for National Geographic Books and is a contributor to the children's magazines *Odyssey*, *Muse*, and *Faces*. When she is not writing about games or the future of technology, she can be found exploring northwestern Montana with a fishing pole or mobile application.

PHOTO CREDITS

Cover baranq/Shutterstock.com; p. 5 © iStockphoto.com/chargerv8; pp. 8–9 betto rodrigues/Shutterstock.com; p. 11 charnsitr/Shutterstock .com; pp. 12–13 Mandy Cheng/AFP/Getty Images; p. 17 Bloomua/ Shutterstock.com; pp. 20–21 © Steve Hamblin/Alamy Stock Photo; pp. 24–25 Monika Wisniewska/Shutterstock.com; p. 27 © AP Images; p. 29 wavebreakmedia/Shutterstock.com; p. 33 Mclek/Shutterstock .com; p. 35 Universal Images Group/Getty Images; pp. 38–39 Dolinsk/ Shutterstock.com; p. 40 © iStockphoto.com/SchulteProductions; pp. 42, 59, 62–63 Monkey Business Images/Shutterstock.com; p. 45 Computer Arts Magazine/Future/Getty Images; p. 49 Diego Cervo/Shutterstock .com; pp. 50–51 Kevork Djansezian/Getty Images; pp. 54–55 Rawpixel .com/Shutterstock.com; p. 57 Chris Ryan/OJO Images/Getty Images; pp. 64–65 The Boston Globe/Getty Images; p. 66 Chesky/Shutterstock.com; back cover and interior pages background image Vladgrin/Shutterstock .com.

Designer: Nicole Russo; Editor: Bernadette Davis; Photo Researcher: Karen Huang